LONDON TROLLEYBUSES

a black and white album

Mick Webber

Capital Transport

Front cover D1 384 was an all Leyland product delivered in April 1936. It received the first Leyland trolleybus body to be supplied to London Transport who bought it to test the durability of the company's bodywork before placing larger orders. It was initially allocated to Bexley depot and is seen in June of that year, about to turn left into London Road, Crayford. Tarred-over tram tracks can be seen in the foreground. 384 was the only Leyland to be fitted with rear wheel spats. The below decks side advert is for Green Line. Note the formidable looking Police box in the background. *PA Photos*

Title page C3 304, an AEC/ BRCW product, seen in a pre-delivery view at the Birmingham factory in May 1936. The rear wheel spats were retained on these vehicles until the end, which in the case of 304 was January 1959. BRCW was to eventually produce 390 bodies for London trolleybuses based on the same type of MCW steel body framework as used by Weymann and Metro-Cammell. *BRCW*

Left The bold image of London Transport is displayed on the north side of Euston Road, King's Cross in July 1939. A B2 class short wheelbase Leyland from Holloway passes on route 613.
London Transport Museum

First published 2009

ISBN 978-1-85414-333-4

Published by Capital Transport Publishing www.capitaltransport.com

Printed by CS Graphics, Singapore

INTRODUCTION

It seems quite amazing that as I write this, approaching nearly 50 years since the end of the London trolleybus system, so many people still crave new material on the subject. Over the last 40 years or more I have constantly pestered, pleaded and generally made a nuisance of myself to libraries, manufacturers, photo agencies and private individuals to uncover photographic gems that might otherwise have remained in dark cupboards. Tracking down some of the official photographs from long since defunct companies has proved difficult and time consuming, but it has been well worth the effort. It has been a rewarding and sometimes costly experience, and some of the fruits of this quest are what you see in this book. The London trolleybus is shown between the years 1931 and 1950, when the system reached its peak. There were just over 1600 trolleybuses scheduled to operate on Monday to Fridays, including the first batch of the latest Q1 design.

Some of the views in this book were originally from glass plates and are therefore of exceptional quality, as are most of the manufacturers views, including some AEC shots that until recently were thought to have been lost forever. The press agencies of Fox, Topical and Hulton were often employed by London Transport to record events during this period, and thankfully these are now all preserved for future generations. A few views of lesser quality have also been included for their rarity value, and I hope that you will agree they are worthy additions.

It is quite apparent from many of these views that the new trolleybuses were very modern in appearance when compared to other vehicles of the time. The gap in ride quality and comfort between them and the trams they replaced was indeed enormous, and it is easy to see why they were so popular with the public. London was one of many undertakings to embrace the trolleybus during the 1930s, as the list of companies rushing to replace its ageing tramways grew. If the temporary operations from Acton and Chiswick are put to one side, the Capital's trolleybuses worked from twenty-one depots, Fulwell being the longest serving at just under thirty-one years; Wandsworth the shortest at just over thirteen years.

When the London Passenger Transport Board was handed the combined tramway undertakings of the London County Council, Metropolitan Electric Tramways, London United Tramways, South Metropolitan, and the local Authorities in 1933, the task of integration and urgent renewal was indeed a formidable one. The Board decided that the trolleybus would be their chosen replacement for the whole of the tramway network, and in just over two years prototypes had been built, orders placed and a start had been made. The costly mammoth operation was to last nearly five years, before the second world war put a stop to the conversions, when nearly the whole of the north London tramway network had been replaced. After hostilities ceased, the trolleybus was no longer the favoured tram replacement and the proposed south London conversion plans were abandoned, the trams being reprieved until the last ones were replaced by diesel buses in 1952.

In these days of noise and pollution, it is a surprise that the trolleybus has not been considered again as a modern means of public transport. The infrastructure costs would be considerably less than that of the modern tram, and we live in hope.

The excellent London Transport Museum must again be thanked for access to their wonderful collection. It seems that just when you think you have seen them all, along comes something else to surprise. This has been a labour of love, and as always with this type of project it would not have been possible without the help and encouragement of others. I must thank Ken Blacker, Peter Horner, Dave Jones, John Shearman, Hugh Taylor and Jim Whiting for their comments, suggestions and help in tracking down some of the views, and for making their collections available. As always, some of the photographs have proved impossible to attribute, and I must therefore offer my sincere apologies to anyone who has not been mentioned.

Of the once massive fleet, nine London trolleybuses still survive preserved in LT colours, plus a further four in Spain (at the last count), and if you need reminding you can still travel on three of them at the East Anglia Transport Museum, and one at the Sandtoft trolleybus museum. Make the trips. If you have any further information or items that could add to future publications, please contact mickwebber@hotmail.com.

Blackheath, June 2009   Mick Webber

The first LUT trolleybus was taken into stock in January 1931, and following on shortly after was No. 2 which was delivered in February. The desolate open surroundings of the UCC factory at Feltham provide the backdrop for this view taken on 16th February 1931 . These vehicles were to become known as 'Diddlers', and the similarity to the Feltham tramcar from the same firm cannot be ignored, especially the treatment of the upper deck front end, and the rounded canopy over the driver's cab. *London Transport Museum*

No. 2 again, and this time it is seen on a trial run on 22nd April 1931. The central headlamp was added in March. During the pre-service test runs it was felt that visibility for the driver was unsatisfactory and later vehicles were fitted with wider windscreens. *R Newell Collection*

Twickenham on the first day, 16th May 1931. Diddlers 4 and 3, decked out with bunting wait for their important guests, watched by a constable. LUT tramcar No. 254 is a W class car built in 1902/3, and later renumbered as London Transport 2528. It was scrapped in August 1935. Although the Kingston routes of the LUT were all converted to trolleybus operation during 1931, the 67 was to remain a tram domain until London Transport days, the change to trolleybuses occurring in October 1935. Out of view, a line up of six more Diddlers are waiting to inaugurate the public service. *BCVM*

It is December 1931, and at Fulwell depot a crowd gathers to inspect the last Diddler, No. 60, complete with white wall tyres. This vehicle was different from the other members of its class in that it had an angled staircase, rather than the straight one fitted to the previous vehicles. This resulted in a 29 upper and 27 lower seating layout rather than a 32/24.

London United Diddler No. 55, delivered in October 1931, pauses in Kingston in the winter of 1931/2 on route 4. Pedestrians seem to be well wrapped up despite the sunshine. These vehicles were classified A1 (1-35) and A2 (36-60), 1-35 having English Electric motors, and the remainder BTH. *BCVM*

No. 34, new in July 1931, waits at the fare stage at Church Road, Teddington, while passengers board to escape the cold for a trip to Kingston or beyond to Tolworth. At this time, the route terminated at Tolworth Red Lion, and although the LUT had obtained powers to extend the route to Tolworth By-pass by way of a loop using Ewell Road and Warren Drive, this did not happen until September 1933 when under LPTB control. The bodies on the Diddlers suffered various structural problems, and No. 34 has already had its curved upper deck window glasses replaced by flat panes with dividing pillars. In this official AEC photograph, the trolleybus overhead has been retouched out. *BCVM*

Eden Street, Kingston is the setting for this rear view of No. 8 on route 1. It is 28th March 1934, and although now in London Transport ownership, the London United livery remains. Apart from the first two, the Diddlers did not have rear blinds, but carried wooden route boards in the lower rear window. It would be another 17 months before the routes would be renumbered into the 600 series. No. 8 served until August 1948.

London United No. 58 gingerly edges through the flooded roadway beneath the Kingston railway bridge on 19th April 1932. The driver is using the clockwise loop wires to avoid the single decker, which appears to be blocking the road. He has just completed an anti-clockwise trip around the Kingston loop, and is heading for the Dittons, one of the backwaters of the system. The trolleybus is only six months old, having been delivered in October 1931, but already the original half-drop window at the front of the upper deck has been replaced by a swivelling unit. *Mirrorpix*

Kingston again, on 9th March 1933, where Diddler No. 3 has been steered into difficulty. The original caption states that it has a puncture, but it seems that the driver has misjudged the roadworks. The booms are down, and help is surely on the way. The original LUT spacing of 18 inches between the wires is evident here. London Transport later increased this to 24 inches. *Mirrorpix*

AEC employed the London News Agency to record London United's No. 61 on 23rd February 1933. "A demonstration was given this morning at Southall, Middlesex, of the newest electric trolleybus, which seats 74 passengers, has a central door and no step, and is to be tried out in London shortly". As shown opposite, it proudly displays the AEC triangle, and, as they provided the electrical equipment, the English Electric symbol also appears. It seated 34 downstairs and 40 upstairs. *AEC*

12

Resplendent No. 61, now with advertisements and blinds fitted, on the AEC test wiring at Southall, shows its modern design off very well in this view, prior to its March 1933 delivery. The London General Omnibus Company built this body at their Chiswick works, but it was to remain unique, as some four months later the LPTB would be formed, and they would have their own plans for the future of the trolleybus. No fleet number was carried and the vehicle never entered London United ownership. It remained the property of AEC, until purchased by London Transport in March 1934. Note the driver's door which opens the opposite way compared with the rest of the fleet. *AEC*

This page and overleaf Three views of London United 61 in the months leading up to the takeover by London Transport in July 1933: one in Kingston, followed closely by a Diddler on the 2, another with passengers boarding in Malden Road, and the third, also on the 4 passing roadworks and redundant covered tram track in Kingston. 61 spent most of its time on the Wimbledon services until the Q1s arrived, when it worked from Hounslow on the 657. Between March and October 1945, it was involved in the Pay as you Board trials from Fulwell on the 604, which included the fitting of a conductor's seat under the stairs. *BCVM*

B2 class Leylands 94-131 were short wheelbase vehicles bodied by Brush. No. 94 is seen here at the company's Loughborough factory on tilt test in September 1935. These were originally built with a half-width bulkhead, but were later modified at Charlton works to incorporate a full width one in 1938. Four hundred and forty one trolleybuses were rebuilt in this way after serious stress problems were discovered. *Brush*

Right Again at the Loughborough works, No. 94 shows her nearside profile, prior to delivery to Fulwell in September 1935. This was the only one of the batch with very deep rear mudguards, the others all being more shallow. All were cut back early in the war to fully reveal the tyres. The B2s were intended for operation at Bexley although a few started at Fulwell on a temporary basis. Increased traffic in the Bexley area saw them transferred to Holloway in 1939 for the quiet Hampstead routes. *Brush*

Two B2s are seen at Loughborough with body shells nearing completion. The date is around August 1935. Deliveries of this class were completed by the end of that year. Brush built 88 trolleybus bodies for London Transport; 38 B2s and 50 of class E1. Their framework, of bolted rather than welded construction, did not prove very durable, and by the outbreak of war the B2s were already proving troublesome. *Brush*

C1 class AEC No. 133, the first trolleybus to be completed with Weymann bodywork is on test at the AEC works at Southall. The date is 1st October 1935, and the vehicle was delivered later that month. The C1s were used to begin trolleybus operation at Fulwell and Hounslow. The bodywork contract for them was divided by the MCW organisation between Weymann and Metro-Cammell, and though there were slight differences, the same C1 class designation was given to both batches. *Getty Images*

C1 class AEC with MCCW bodywork No. 175 was delivered in October 1935, just one day before C1s inaugurated routes 657 and 667 on the 27th of that month. The vehicle is recorded here at Hammersmith, Beadon Road, about to turn into King Street. This vehicle was later one of five sold for further service to Georgetown Municipal Transport in Malaya in 1956. It survived there until November 1959. *London Transport Museum*

Right C1 No. 156 waits outside Hounslow depot on the 657, about to be joined by a sister vehicle which appears to be emerging from a temporarily wired up yard at the side of the new depot, which is still not yet fully operational. Vehicles leaving eastbound would do so via a trailing frog, and westbound they would have their poles changed from a dead end wire to the main line. Workmen are still busy putting the finishing touches to the new building, and a man on a ladder is in attendance to work on a traction standard. People gather to witness the new service, and the entrance columns to the old tram depot on the left will soon be gone. It is possibly the first day of service, which was 27th October 1935. *PA Photos*

23

180 was a Metro-Cammell bodied C1 class vehicle, and it waits at the Hammersmith Grove stand of route 667 with ST 90 on the 27 for company. Starting in a small way before the war, but mostly after, the small side lights positioned between decks within the cream band were replaced on the majority of C1s with the more conventional lights side mounted below the cab windows. *AEC*

The only four-wheeler in the fleet was No. 63, which was an AEC/English Electric product purchased in 1934 for evaluation purposes. It lost out to the six-wheel prototype No. 62 and therefore remained unique. 63 is seen at Hampton Court on route 604. It was transferred to Hounslow when the Q1s arrived; it was withdrawn in June 1952. The four piece front indicator display, which was fitted to the vehicle when it was still very new, was never fully utilised. The rear wheel spats, a later addition, were removed round about the outbreak of war. *C.Martin c/o Kevin Lane*

Above November 10th 1935 was the first day of service 698. Its sister route the 696 was to follow on 24th November. B2 No. 110, a Brush bodied Leyland, turns at Woolwich Free Ferry for a return trip to Bexleyheath. Note the main tram wire crossing the trolleybus overhead. This cramped terminus would remain until July 1943, when a short extension to a more spacious stand at Parsons Hill would be opened. These short-wheelbased 60-seaters would soon prove inadequate for the traffic on the Bexley routes, and they were replaced by 70 seaters. *London Transport Museum*

Left B2 No. 96 poses with smartly turned out driver and conductor under the watchful eye of a seated Inspector. The stop sign is attached to a new traction standard, which stands by a feeder pillar, and is unusually sited on a corner. The official London Transport and Leyland photographers were much in evidence during these early days, and the date is probably sometime during November 1935. *London Transport Museum*

A modern motorist's dream: an empty street in London. Goldhawk Road is remarkably quiet in this view with only two cyclists and one parked car sharing the road with C1 class trolleybus No. 154 from Hounslow depot on the 657. Street lights are provided on one side of the road only and are suspended from an overhead wire attached to the traction standards. *Stilltime Photos*

Right Leyland/Brush B2 class No. 95 arrived in September 1935 and features in Leyland's official views taken on 28th February 1936. It is seen passing the main Woolwich Arsenal gate on route 698. The road has since been re-aligned and now runs behind this structure, which is now a listed building. The body on this vehicle was destroyed on 7th November 1940 after a bomb fell on Bexley depot. The chassis was lengthened to 30ft, and a new body supplied by Weymann in 1941. It was reclassified D2A and renumbered 95A. *BCVM*

B1 class Leyland/BRCW No. 76 came in December 1935 and was delivered to Sutton for the 654 route. This class of 60-seaters remained on the 654 until its demise in 1959. It is seen navigating the new roundabout at Crystal Palace with one of the two 275ft high towers in the background. The date is 28th February 1936 and the Palace had less than a year to go; it was destroyed by fire on November 30th. The towers lasted until the war, when it was felt they provided too good a location marker for enemy aircraft and were therefore demolished. *BCVM*

Bexleyheath Broadway in April 1936, and Brush bodied, Leyland B2 60 seater No. 106, passes MCCW bodied AEC C1 70 seater No.175, giving us an all-round view of a basically similar design that was a vast contrast to the trams they had just replaced. The AEC was one of the vehicles recently drafted in to ease the overcrowding on route 696.
London Transport Museum

Acton depot operated trolleybuses briefly between April 1936 and March 1937 only, and this was for operational convenience. Although a poor quality view, this rare shot shows a C2 class trolleybus emerging from the depot on to the High Street. The depot had been previously owned by London United Tramways. *Mick Webber Collection*

Right The first B1, No. 64, stands at Sutton depot in the summer of 1936. The driver proudly wears his summer white coat, and both crew members have their white cap covers on. Staff were obliged to wear these between May 1st and September 30th. The B1s spent most of their working lives at Sutton, which in the case of No. 64 was until May 1955. *Mick Webber Collection*

Bexleyheath was the only new purpose built trolleybus depot on a new site. It can be seen on November 7th 1935, just three days before commencement of new route 698, the sister route 696 not starting until the 24th. The vehicles on display are all B2s numbered 94, 103, 99 and 112. *London Transport Museum*

Walthamstow trams had terminated at the Ferry Boat Inn in Forest Road travelling in from the east on route 23, and the link further along to Tottenham High Road, although authorised, had never been built. This gap was finally bridged on 18th October 1936, when new trolleybus route 623 was introduced. Seen on the first day of service is C3 class No. 367, an AEC with bodywork by the Birmingham Railway Carriage and Wagon Company. 367's conductor has yet to grasp the niceties of blind changing, as the vehicle is not showing Tottenham Hale, its intended destination. *Getty Images*

Tram route 21 was originally a joint LCC/MET route introduced in November 1913 between Holborn and North Finchley. London Transport inherited the route in July 1933, and it continued until 5/6th March 1938, when it was replaced by trolleybuses on routes 521 and 621. C3 class AEC No 311 was delivered in June 1936, and is seen on the 621 in the period just before the outbreak of war. The freshly tarred over tram tracks are clearly evident. The vehicle has just left Manor House and is proceeding along Green Lanes.
Michael Wickham collection

GOLDHAWK ROAD. W.

No: 3934

This commercial postcard view shows Goldhawk Road, with C1 class Weymann bodied 133 on route 657. It was delivered in October 1935. London trolleybuses ceased carrying upper deck rear advertising before the war.

Right C1 148 pauses on route 657 in the summer of 1936 at Kew Bridge. Another C class vehicle is behind on the 667 with a smartly dressed young couple strolling past, perhaps about to board for the trip to Hampton Court. Others are alighting, and some will no doubt be on their way to Kew Gardens. A distant trolleybus is turning short on the wire provided here for vehicles travelling from the east. A feeder pillar complete with LT telephone, enamel signs, a conductors' time clock and a phone box all add to this evocative scene.
G H F Atkins

37

November 1936, and heavy rain has caused flooding in Acton. Metro-Cammell bodied Leyland D2 404 carefully negotiates the waters on route 607, which had only been introduced on the 15th of that month. It is working short to Southall, Delamere Road. All of the D2s at Hanwell were replaced by F1s in 1937, having proved insufficiently powerful to keep to the exacting schedule of route 607. *London Borough of Ealing*

Chiswick High Road, outside David Greig's offices, in 1936. The grocery firm's shops were once a familiar name on most High Streets. C1 140 is on route 657, followed by STL 697 on the 32 and a Green Line T on route N. The STL would have just started its journey at Turnham Green, while the Green Line had travelled from Windsor. *London Transport Museum*

Shepherd's Bush Green, and MCCW bodied C1 146 is seen in a splendid panned shot on route 657 in December 1936. The vehicle is just over a year old, and appears to be in the safe hands of the local constabulary! The early rear wheel covers, which were modified before and just after the outbreak of war, stand out in this view. Note that the side blind includes a bracketed Spring Grove. *London Transport Museum*

This page and opposite The E2 class were a batch of 25 AECs with Weymann bodies and were delivered between April and June 1937. These three views were taken during construction at Weymann's factory at Addlestone earlier that year. They were to spend their working lives at West Ham. The bodies, which employed MCW patented steel frames, proved very durable, and were largely trouble free throughout their working lives, which exceeded twenty years. These vehicles were fitted with full width bulkheads from new, as can be seen in the photograph on the right. Three of the class had their bodies destroyed during the war and were subsequently rebodied, one by Weymann and the other two by Northern Coachbuilders. *Weymann*

E2 No. 606 was delivered in April 1937. Weymann built the body on an AEC chassis, and the vehicle, as all of its class, was allocated to West Ham where it remained until withdrawal in February 1960. Weymann bodies could be distinguished from all others by their rear domes, which were formed in three pieces rather than a single unit. *Weymann*

E2 606 is the subject again here in this mystery shot at Earls Court. It is presumably April 1937, the month in which it was delivered; it is being towed by a six-wheel AEC unit, probably from Southall as it has a Middlesex trade plate. The exhibition centre did not open until September of that year, and there is still a lot of building work being done, so the purpose of its visit is unknown. The Commercial Vehicle Show did not take place until November 1937, by which time 606 would have been seven months old, and it is not in the list of vehicles that appeared that year. Possibly it was there for clearance checks before the big event so that a place could be reserved for a similar vehicle.

Tramway Avenue, Stratford is the location of this view, and E2 No. 610 is on route 699 bound for the Docks. This was the first route to commence the West Ham services on 6th June 1937. This vehicle spent nearly 23 years in the East End, and was withdrawn in February 1960, leaving West Ham with just three months of trolleybus operation left. *Mick Webber Collection*

Park Royal bodied the E3 class AECs, which were easily recognisable from the front by the four rows of vents between decks. E3 No. 646 is on the Silvertown Way on route 669 bound for Stratford Broadway. The driver shows to advantage the ability of the trolleybus to avoid the roadworks, and the trolley booms are extended almost to their maximum as he swings the vehicle around the obstruction. The Park Royal bodies of this class did not wear as well as their contemporaries and, apart from the rebodied vehicles, all had been withdrawn by October 1956. *Mick Webber Collection*

A trolleybus from Bexley ends up in several front gardens in Wickham Lane after a mishap on the 696 sometime in 1937. It appears to have been hit on the offside by another vehicle. Note the position of the trolley booms. No doubt Charlton Works would sort it out, but meanwhile the local residents have plenty to talk about. *Getty Images*

Brush of Loughborough show off their product, E1 No. 570, in June 1937 just prior to delivery later that month. It turned out to be an early withdrawal, lasting only until May 1955. Brush's records show the body weight to be 3 tons 10cwt, and the E1 bodies deteriorated quickly, requiring many of them to be heavily rebuilt at Chiswick tram depot in the early post-war years. The E1s commenced service at Walthamstow, Ilford and West Ham and did not stray elsewhere until well into the post-war era. *Brush*

Leyland were very proud to be awarded the order for the 100 F1 class trolleybuses, for which they also built the bodywork. On 18th June 1937 their cameraman captured 665 on tow with the works lorry, presumably ready for delivery. The first ten F1s, 654–663, were built with half width bulkheads, but the remainder had full width as can be seen in this view. *BCVM*

F1 697 was posed in Leyland's inspection shop on 30th June 1937, with 23 years of service ahead of it. It was delivered to London Transport on 24th July. Leyland bodies proved to be the sturdiest of all, but although the F1s served extremely well at Hanwell depot, they were not universally popular, because of the non-standard (for London) electrical specification, which called for a belt driven generator for lighting, instead of the tried and tested motor generator. *BCVM*

Clapham Junction late in 1937 and Hammersmith based D2 class Leyland 423 is on route 628 passing 1906 vintage E class tram No. 628 on route 26. The 26 had been replaced in part by route 626, and was due to be replaced in full in the South London tram to trolleybus conversions, which were later suspended due to the outbreak of war. After the war, plans were changed, and diesel buses replaced the remaining tram routes. 423 had been delivered in October 1936 initially to Hanwell depot and remained in stock until 1959. Tram 628 was scrapped at Walthamstow in March 1938. *Capital Transport Collection*

Leyland's paint shop had a visit from the Fox Photos cameraman on 20th October 1937. He recorded an unidentified F1 being prepared for its final paint job before its delivery later that year. Leyland was the only supplier of trolleybus bodies to London to employ spray painting. All of the class were in stock by the end of December and all entered service at Hanwell, where many of them stayed until that depot's conversion to buses in November 1960. *Getty Images*

D2 No. 400 had been delivered in October 1936, and it is seen at West Croydon in a photograph taken for the British Electrical Development Association. The date is 8th October 1937 and it is about to pass a B class vehicle on route 654, which is preceded by another trolleybus showing a 'special' display. Number 400's blind is set for its return journey to 'Nr Willesden Junction' which is a quaint description for Scrubs Lane. It is followed by a country area front entrance STL. *Barry Turner Collection*

E1 class 556 travels along High Road Leyton on route 697 bound for the Docks in late 1937. The vehicle and the route were new in May and June of that year respectively. Tram track is being removed as trams on various routes along here had been withdrawn on June 6th. The busy Baker's Arms junction is in the background. *Mick Webber Collection*

F1 735 arrived in London from Leyland's on 18th October 1937, and it is seen at the factory on the 12th of that month. The whole class was initially delivered to Hanwell where it took over routes 607 and 655. The F1s were to remain a familiar sight on these routes along with Bank Holiday specials on the 657 and 667. The 95hp motors in these vehicles were noticeably more powerful than those in the D2s that they replaced. *BCVM*

The London Transport official photographer visited Finchley depot in November 1937 and captured C2 No. 199 having its evening wash. For an unknown reason, a front route blind is not in position. The rear wheel spats on these vehicles were easily removed for maintenance. No. 199's nearside opening windscreen has been replaced by a fixed pane of glass to give greater rigidity, and within a few months a full width bulkhead will be fitted. *London Transport Museum*

Opposite: Apart from 952 (which was constructed by Metro-Cammell) the J1 class were AEC vehicles with Weymann bodies. No. 952 was delivered to London Transport in December 1937, but before that it appeared at the Commercial Vehicle Show at London's Earls Court in November (4th–13th). This was the first such show at the new venue, which opened on 1st September with the Chocolate and Confectionery show. Previous shows had been held at nearby Olympia. The Commercial shows were biennial, and this was the last show to be put on until 1948. Two views show 952 being positioned on the MCW stand by a tractor. The rear view is of particular interest as it shows the unladen weight and legal lettering on the offside of the vehicle, in addition to the nearside which was the normal practice.

METROPOLITAN-CAMMELL CARRIAGE & WAGON C.º L.ᵀᴰ
Metropolitan Road, Saltley, Birmingham, 8.

61

70-seater Double-Deck Rear Entrance Trolley-Bus, Mounted on A.E.C. 6-Wheel Electric Chassis.

M.C.W. patented metal construction, embodying tubular pillar section and steel lining sheets, rivetted together to form a complete inner skin; side panels in aluminium alloy; roof, facia and canopy panels in 18G aluminium; screws securing panels and mouldings electro-galvanised; bicycle rail fixed along bottom edge of rear panel; rear enclosed platform; emergency exit in upper saloon at rear end by outward opening window hinged at bottom, with stainless steel 3-point locking gear and fittings; emergency exit in lower saloon arranged by setting back the rear nearside pillar 1 ft. 6 in. (clear) to comply with M.O.T. regulations; staircase of right-angled type, with stringers and risers of 18G. H.S.T. alloy and elm treads; floors of upper saloon covered in oak slatting secured by galvanised wood screws; floor in lower saloon covered linoleum; 13 Widney Stuart halfdrop windows with stainless steel fittings, viz., 10 at sides, 2 at front bulkhead of upper saloon and 1 at nearside front bulkhead in lower saloon, these bulkhead lights being glazed in triplex toughened safety glass; emergency exit window in upper saloon glazed in triplex sheet safety glass; all main windows fitted into special pressed steel window frames; full-fronted type driver's compartment, with unit type screen with Auster latest type quadrants-frames, painted finish, with quadrants and fittings chromium plated and glazed in laminated safety plate quality glass; sliding and fixed side windows in compartment glazed in safety sheet glass; cab door fitted at offside; driver's seat of Leveroll-Leverex pattern with cushion of hairlock and springs with Xetal squab and trimmed rexine; illuminated destination boxes, showing service number and destinations at front and rear; route indicators, showing names of route at nearside over step; Eco heavy duty gears fitted in both destination and route number boxes; stencil type service number plates on near and offside of body; seats made up on Accles & Pollock tubular frames, of chrome molybdenum steel tube, sandblasted rust-proofed and stone enamelled; cushions and squabs of "Dunlopillo"; cushions and squabs in upper saloon trimmed in L.P.T.B. blue moquette, edges covered in leather to match; cushions and squabs in lower saloon trimmed in L.P.T.B. green moquette, edges covered in leather to match; ventilation by continuous metal louvres over all side windows and front of upper deck; "Novobax" intake ventilator fitted at front end of upper saloon; air intake in the lower deck over nearside cab windscreen with duct through cab to bulkhead, with distributing baffle on the saloon side; two super Ashanco extractors in upper saloon, with stainless steel grids and secured by stainless steel screws; ventilation of driver's compartment effected by intake over offside windscreen; illumination of saloons by 28 lamps of the white bakelite open reflector type with 50 m.m. opal bulbs; "Taw" head lamps, side lamps, rear lamp and stop lamp.

Woodwork and lining panels covered rexine to L.P.T.B. shades; ceiling in lower saloon of plywood with aluminium cornice panels—enamelled finish; ceiling and cornice panels of upper saloon of aluminium, enamelled finish; platform handpole and commodes covered white doverite, all insulated to comply with M.O.T. regulations; staircase handrails, stanchions and window guards in polished alloy; miscellaneous equipment and fittings include front and rear wings of rubber, detachable rear shrouds, floor draining ferrules, concertina type blind, inside drivers' compartment, advertisement frames, electric bell and buzzer, notice frames, "used" ticket box, staircase mirror, 3 driving mirrors, bulb horn, electric horn, recessed rear registration plate, detachable platform with chains and fittings for fixing outside emergency window, two C.A.V. Bosch windscreen wipers, etc.; finished in red, cream and aluminium roofs.

Price complete as shown, £2,925.

M1 class 953 was a lightweight unit-constructed vehicle with Weymann bodywork, new in February 1938. It was the first vehicle to feature radiused front upper deck windows and incorporated a one-piece front destination screen, unique in the fleet. It was also the only vehicle to be fitted with AEC's decorative front wheel trims. Although it was fitted with a plain front removable panel on delivery, the view here at the AEC works shows it with a standard panel complete with louvres. J1 930 stands next to it in this view. 953 had a short life, however, as it was burnt out during the war. *AEC*

This second shot of 953 is after delivery to Fulwell for pre-service checks. It displays a 641 route stencil along with a 667 side blind display. It was common for any available displays to be fitted for an official photo, whether they agreed with each other or not. Here, 953 is kept company by H1 797, which is also there to be commissioned for service. Note the all-red roof on 953. Former LUT No. 61 can be seen on the left just inside the depot. *AEC*

People gather to inspect H1 class No. 796 at Kings Cross in February 1938, prior to commencement of new services on 6th March. In the summer of 1939, this trolleybus, along with many other H1s at Holloway, was transferred to Bexley depot, where it stayed until March 1959. A further transfer took it to Walthamstow depot from where this Leyland MCCW vehicle was withdrawn and presented to the Paris Transport Museum. *Stilltime Photos*

Taken on the same day, 796 again seen this time at Holborn whilst traversing the loop with a few chosen travellers sampling the new mode of transport. The driver waits patiently in traffic behind an STL and taxis wait for trade. Gamage's store, a delight for children of all ages, is holding a sale to celebrate 60 years of business. *Stilltime Photos*

J2 960 was an AEC/BRCW product new in February 1938. It was sent to Finchley to commence new services on 6th March and it is seen on that day on route 521 on Bounds Green Road. To signify which way 960 would traverse the Holborn loop, Grays Inn Road is portrayed in the same size lettering as Holborn Circus. This was the first time that route numbers used the 500 series. It saw service for 22 years, being withdrawn in February 1960. *Dave Jones Collection*

North Finchley was a busy trolleybus terminus which also included two through routes to Barnet, the 609 and 645. Holloway's H1 class 806 is seen in March 1938 when only one month old, passing a Leyland Cub rescue lorry which was numbered 222 in the pre-war series and had been delivered to Finchley depot in October 1936. These and their Albion counterparts were a common sight throughout the system and this one (renumbered 207c) remained in stock until June 1962. The H1's tenure at Holloway was short lived. Many were transferred two months later to Wood Green, and others to Bexley in 1939. *Photomatic*

Wood Green began trolleybus operation on 8th May 1938. It received a large batch of new and used H1s, mainly for new routes 629 and 641. Tucked away at the back of the depot, vehicles are stored in readiness for the conversion. The ADC tram breakdown tender awaits its fate. During the early days of this conversion, some vehicles were initially housed at Holloway. *D W K Jones*

H1 class trolleybuses 821 and 842 photographed around May 1938. The class had a long association with Wood Green depot, though they did operate elsewhere. Both of these vehicles were withdrawn in April 1959. Metro-Cammell bodywork was the most common on London trolleybuses, the company being responsible for 764 in total. *D. Evans Collection, The Omnibus Society*

H1 class 756 and 770 are among the line up of brand-new trolleybuses at Holloway depot in March 1938, prior to the conversion on the 6th of that month. No. 756 displays a route blind for the 671, a route that was planned but never introduced. It was originally to have been shared between Holloway and Hackney depots, and was later to emerge as the 555 in June 1939. The third vehicle in the line up also displays a route that was never to be, the 537. Together with the 637, these two route numbers were included on the Holloway blinds as routes that were planned to operate the Hampstead and Parliament Hill Fields services, but which never materialised. *Getty Images*

It is March 1938 and route 621 has just commenced. Seen in Holloway Road, a J class vehicle waits patiently whilst crowds board and alight from HR/2 class tram No. 140 on route 11. This car was built in 1931, and was to survive until March 1952. Another tram on Subway route 35 is waiting its turn in the queue. Tram route 11 would be replaced by trolleybuses in December 1939. A smart delivery boy on his bicycle waits on the cobblestones at the red light. *London Borough of Islington*

BRCW built the bodies for the AEC J2 class, with 975 being delivered in March 1938. It is seen at the Birmingham factory before delivery. Note the straight gutter fitted above the rear upper window which distinguished these from otherwise very similar bodies by Metro-Cammell. This vehicle remained in stock until April 1960. The trolleybus bullseye transfer positioned alongside the rear number plate was moved early in the war, and displayed on the lower rear window. *BRCW*

All-Leyland F1 No. 668 is seen at Kew Bridge on route 655. The vehicle had arrived in June 1937, though the route commenced in December 1936. It is unclear what the driver is doing here; the Kew Bridge turn was wired up for trolleybuses travelling from the east. *G O P Pearce*

North Finchley terminus on 17th June 1938. J1 class 916 is on route 617, and on the 609 is H1 801. The Metro-Cammell body on 801 was damaged beyond repair on 29th June 1944, when a flying bomb hit Bexley depot, and the vehicle was later rebodied by East Lancs. *G O P Pearce*

Hampstead tram depot was closed on 10th July 1938, when its trams were replaced by trolleybuses operating from nearby Holloway. Two months later, on 12th September, J2 992 is captured at King's Cross. The delights of the Green Line service were widely advertised at the time. This was Holloway's second round of new routes, the depot having received its first trolleybuses in March of that year. *G O P Pearce*

The British Aluminium Company ran a series of advertisements boasting of the virtues of using their product in vehicle manufacture. Two of these featured London trolleybuses, as shown here with B1 class 89 and C1 class Nos 133, 135 and 170, from the July and October 1938 issues of the Australian magazine 'Transportation'.

Leyland's largest order for London Transport trolleybuses was for the K1 and K2 classes. There were 300 of these all-Leyland buses delivered between September 1938 and June 1939. K2 1158 is seen in the finishing shops on 16th September 1938. It was withdrawn in July 1960, though it remained in stock until April 1961. London Transport stipulated that exterior advertisement panels should be left unvarnished for better adhesion of the paper advertising bills. *Getty Images*

The AEC works at Southall is the setting for this view of new J3s 1054 and 1052. These had BRCW bodywork and were the last J3s delivered, arriving in October 1938. No. 1054 was supplied with a modified and more streamlined front dome which was perpetuated on BRCWs next order for the N1 class. 1054 was later to meet with the Kentish Town railway bridge in November 1960, causing the vehicle's immediate withdrawal. *AEC*

Leyland's body erection shop is the scene on 31st October 1938, as lower and upper decks start to near completion. Leyland manufactured the K1 and K2 classes, which differed only in their electrical equipment; the K1s having Metrovick control equipment and the K2s English Electric. Curiously each deck was painted separately before being fitted together. *BCVM*

Leyland's factory premises on 28th December 1938. Works lorry No. 3 has K1 1127 on tow, presumably ready for delivery to the capital, where it arrived the following day. No. 1127 was destined to spend its life working from Stamford Hill depot. *BCVM*

To enable a target date of 16th October 1938 to be met for a tram to trolleybus changeover at Edmonton depot, it was necessary to beg borrow or steal trolleybuses from other depots until such time that enough K types were delivered. H1 class 819 had been brought in from Walthamstow, and is seen at Mount Pleasant on route 659 in the winter of 1938/9. The driver has not been bothered to use his headlights despite the bad weather, and is no doubt looking forward to a short break at the stand in a few minutes. *Stilltime Photos*

Fortunately for us, the official photographer was very busy during the manufacture of the K class trolleybuses. Their works lorry is hitched up to K1 1285 on 25th February 1939, according to the photographer's record book. It is blinded up and ready to go, as a rather wooden looking policeman looks on. London Transport recorded it as having been taken into stock the previous month. No. 1285 suffered severe bomb damage in Leyton on 11th October 1940; it was subsequently rebodied by Weymann and renumbered 1285A. *BCVM*

In the very early days of route 629, Wood Green's J2 987 is seen just south of the depot, with an unidentified STL on route 29. AEC trolleybuses such as this, spent only a short time at Wood Green before the depot was fully stocked with H1 class Leylands. *Dave Jones Collection*

1555 was numerically the first of the ninety N1 class AECs bodied by BRCW. This splendid works view of the nearside taken in May 1939 shows the handsome lines of the London trolleybus very well. Note the absence of the route number stencil holder above the last lower deck window, and the provision for a new one below the same window. This vehicle started life at Bow depot. *BRCW*

Top left London Transport had a trolleybus specially built for use in the Kingsway tram subway. Class X5 No. 1379 was constructed with offside doors to facilitate use of the loading islands in the subway but, after trials on 13th August 1939, was found to be unsuitable. It spent all of its life at Holloway depot between June 1939 and March 1955 and is seen during the war on route 653. *D Evans Collection, Omnibus Society*

Left Finchley's C3 320 on route 621. Wartime blackout masks adorn the headlamps, and what looks like fresh white paint has been applied to the mudguards. Pedestrians dutifully carry their gas masks in this scene at Jolly Butchers Hill in Wood Green. *D Evans Collection, Omnibus Society*

Above Prototype London Transport six-wheeler No. 62 was an AEC/MCCW vehicle delivered to the Board in July 1934 for evaluation trials alongside the four-wheel No. 63. It was allocated to Fulwell and is seen during the war at Hampton Court on route 667. It went to Holloway in 1948, where it stayed until withdrawn in September 1952. *W J Haynes*

L1 class chassisless trolleybus 1367 has had its MCCW bodywork severely damaged in an accident. This shot was taken at Charlton Works on 5th July 1940. Many accidents happened as a result of the blackout restrictions and this may well have been the case in this instance.
London Transport Museum

Brentford Half Acre was a short working for trolleybuses on routes 655, 657 and 667. One of Hanwell's trusty F1s, 735, is seen during the war years in St Paul's Road. The advert hopes to encourage war savings.
W J Haynes

K1 1096 is on route 649 and is travelling along Waltham Cross High Street, as the local Home Guard march past saluting as they go. Both trolleybuses have a white blackout strip painted at the rear. *London Borough of Enfield*

The vehicles forming the SA1, 2 and 3 classes were all 8ft wide trolleybuses diverted to London Transport instead of their intended customers in South Africa; this was due to wartime shipping restrictions. Vehicles were in short supply and LT were grateful for anything that became available. They were all allocated to Ilford depot, where they spent their entire lives. SA1 No. 1722, a Leyland/MCCW product, is seen on 21st November 1941 after leaving the Perth Road exit of Ilford depot. The darkened upper window top sections can clearly be seen. These were to guard against the strong South African sun, hardly a problem in Ilford! *Topical Press*

Far left B2 class 108's Brush body has suffered blast damage and is parked here in Holloway depot awaiting attention on 17th October 1940. Winston Churchill reminds the public that they deserve victory, a message aimed at boosting morale after the blitz suffered that year. *London Transport Museum.*

Farringdon Road in 1941 and bomb-damaged buildings surround Finchley depot's J2 class No. 969 as it edges forward on route 517. A number of its windows have been blown out, and temporary boarding has enabled the trolleybus to be put straight back into service. LT maintenance crews were often enlisted to help demolish or make safe damaged buildings that could pose a hazard to tram or trolleybus routes.
Mick Webber Collection

West Croydon is the setting for this wartime view of D3 No. 548 on route 630. This bus is sporting all of the wartime additions, including the anti-blast window netting. The driver was allowed 74 minutes for the journey to Scrubs Lane.
W J Haynes

D2 430 was bomb damaged at West Ham works on 30th July 1944, and was sent to Northern Coachbuilders for rebodying after the war. The bodies were similar to the N1 class, although they were wooden framed and had a full height entrance. It was captured by the official photographer in Newcastle before its trip south; its trolley poles were fitted after arrival in London. *Northern Coachbuilders*

D2 385 was also a victim of the war, this time a flying bomb incident at Bexley on 29th June 1944. Northern Coachbuilders again supplied the new body, and it was photographed in January 1946 as 385C before being despatched to London, again minus trolley poles. Out of the 20 new bodies supplied by NCB, ten were returned without seats and this was one of them. *Northern Coachbuilders*

Another rebodied vehicle was 391B, which was damaged at Bexley on 29th June 1944. In this case, East Lancs were chosen to supply the new body, which was one of 25, and the result is seen here. It is Bexleyheath Broadway, during a heavy snowfall in February 1948, and according to the press caption at the time, "the poles were frozen to the wires".
Kentish Times

SA3 No. 1760 was an AEC/MCCW vehicle delivered in February 1943. The side vents between decks, intended for a much hotter climate, are clearly visible, as is the front sliding door, which was panelled over and never used. All the SA class vehicles seated 72, rather than the more common 70 seats on the standard fleet. *Eric Munday*

The new order. BUT/MCCW supplied the post-war trolleybuses to London Transport. They were intended to replace the ageing Diddlers and the vehicles destroyed during the hostilities. The deliveries came in two batches, in 1948/9 and in 1952/3. Q1 class No. 1779 is on tilt test at the Metro-Cammell factory in January 1948, the month in which it was delivered. The whole of this batch was sent to Fulwell. *MCW*

Q1 No. 1766 pauses at Tolworth Red Lion in February 1948; it is on driver familiarisation duties from Fulwell depot. The fact that it displays a running number plate indicates that it has already seen service. The Q1s were of five-bay construction and were eight feet wide with concealed trolley gantries. *Eric Munday*

It is June 1948 and Q1 1813 is seen at the MCCW factory at Elmdon in Birmingham in a non-professional photograph possibly taken by a member of staff or a visitor. It will soon be on its way to Fulwell depot for pre-service checks. It was sold to Pontevedra in Spain in 1961 and delivered to Vigo. It was never used, and remained in LT condition until broken up in 1977.

In a photograph probably taken by the same photographer, Q1 1812 is seen with 1807 and 1775 at the MCCW Birmingham factory prior to their delivery in September 1948. This vehicle was sold to Santander-Astillero in Spain in 1961 and remained in service until December 1974. The British Trolleybus Society purchased it for preservation in May 1977 and it was shipped back to England, arriving on 19th June 1977. After storage, it arrived at Sandtoft in 1979 and was in due course restored to its original condition, making its debut to the public in 2001.

Hampton Court is the setting for Q1 1791 during the summer of 1948. These trolleybuses must have seemed complete luxury to the travelling public who were used to riding on the Diddlers in the area. Note the front adverts urging everyone to save water. Nothing new. *S L Poole*

Q1 1801 was only a few months old when captured at Shannon Corner on the 604. It is 22nd June 1948 and it retains its gleaming good looks as it heads for Hampton Court on a fine sunny day. *Denis Battams, LCCTT*

In January 1945, C3 378 was a victim of war damage in Freemasons Road, West Ham; it was rebuilt as a Pay-as-you-Board trolleybus along with No 61. The experiments on route 604 were between November 1945 and March 1946, when the special equipment was removed. Its staircase had been repositioned, hence the missing offside window. It is recorded at Golders Green, working a short on the 660. Its non-standard status caused it to be withdrawn from Isleworth on 31st May 1952, although it was used as a trainer until December 1953. *Dewi Williams*

The war-damaged trolleybuses that were rebodied by Weymann were not a success. Unlike the East Lancs and Northern Coachbuilders products, these were built during the war, when in a lot of cases sub-standard materials were used. This resulted in their early deterioration and as a result London Transport was forced to seek urgent measures to find a solution. Mann Egerton of Norwich was awarded the contract to rebuild them during 1949. The ribbed roof and sliding ventilators were the main distinguishing features of the Weymann bodies. 1565A is seen prior to the rebuild, when allocated to Fulwell on the 604 at Hampton Court. Diddler 52 is behind. *Don Thompson*

The Topical Press Agency was enlisted to take photographs on 17th March 1949 to show commercial advertising positions on a trolleybus. K1 class 1120 was used to display front adverts and was parked at Stamford Hill depot. *London Transport Museum*

K3 class No. 1690 suffered damage in May 1949 when it ended up in a garden in New Road, Edmonton. It was on the 649, although the nearside route stencil shows 659. It was the first K3 to be withdrawn, being so in September 1958. The breakdown crew in attendance have arrived in one of the four breakdown tenders to be converted from former LS class double-deck buses, which can be seen on the left. *Getty Images*

Q1 1832 is in Kingston on route 602 during 1948. These vehicles seemed wasted on these quiet routes, and would surely have been of more use on some of the busier trunk routes on the system. This trolleybus ended its days in Zaragoza in Spain, where it saw service from 1961 until 1975. It was last known as a children's nursery in Barcelona in 1978. *Alan Cross*

H1 786 was a casualty on 29th June 1944, when Bexley depot received a direct hit from a flying bomb. East Lancs supplied its new body. Now numbered 786B, it is waiting at Woolwich Parsons Hill in 1948, ready to depart for Dartford, with a front offside mudguard badly in need of attention. *Alan Cross*

Twin-steering Leyland 1671 is seen on route 607, complete with damaged side panel. Note the positioning of the running number plate. The vehicle was registered in Lancashire, as it was originally owned by Leyland; It joined London Transport as a demonstrator in May 1939, and received the fleet number 1671 when it was purchased in September of the same year. It lasted until May 1955. *Mick Webber Collection*

Diddler No 37 waits at Wimbledon Town Hall on route 604, with C1 class 171 for company. A new Q1 is just visible in the distance, making up the three generations of London trolleybus. The two vehicles display advertisements for Bentalls, the large departmental store in Kingston. The first offside lower front panel on number 37, which included the driver's step, has been removed. The C1s were at Fulwell for the 667 but also made appearances on the Diddler routes.

A post-war view of a Diddler. Its service days now numbered, No. 32 pulls away from the stop at Malden on route 604, just passing under the frog for the short turn back towards Kingston. The practice of boarding up war damaged houses with advertising hoardings is illustrated well. *F J Reynolds*

A rear view of Kingsway subway trolleybus 1379, seen on 5th August 1950 alongside T 655 working Green Line 723 to Grays. It is waiting time at Aldgate on the 653. The offside entrance gives the vehicle a curious rear profile, and the inside layout resulted in a loss of one seat on each deck, bringing the total capacity down to 68. Bow's 1644 can be seen on the right on route 661. *Alan Cross*